MOZAMBIQUE 2016 HUMAN RIGHTS REPORT

EXECUTIVE SUMMARY

Mozambique is a multiparty parliamentary democracy with a freely elected republican form of government. The most recent national elections for president, parliament, and provincial assemblies took place in October 2014. Voters elected Filipe Nyusi of the ruling Front for the Liberation of Mozambique (Frelimo) party as president. Multiple national and international observers considered voting generally orderly but lacking transparency during vote tabulation. Some domestic and foreign observers and local civil society organizations expressed concern over election irregularities such as delays in observer credentialing, excessive numbers of invalid votes, and inordinately high voter turnout in some districts, which they alleged indicated ballot box stuffing.

Civilian authorities at times did not maintain effective control over security forces.

The country experienced significant domestic upheaval during the year due to the continuing armed conflict between government Defense and Security Forces (FDS) and militarized members of the main opposition party, the Mozambique National Resistance (Renamo). Confrontations between the government and Renamo, which the Mozambican Human Rights League (LDH) termed "a low intensity civil war," increased in rural areas of the central and northwestern parts of the country and contributed to more than 10,000 persons fleeing to Malawi. There were reports of abuses committed by the FDS. The conflict included several retaliatory kidnappings and killings of Renamo and Frelimo officials. In May local residents discovered an alleged mass grave near the border between Manica and Sofala Provinces. Although the government blocked access to the site, reporters found approximately a dozen corpses scattered in the bush nearby. A reported second mass gravesite was later found close by. While a parliamentary investigative team did not come to any definitive conclusions or hold the government responsible, it was the first time such an investigative committee was formed.

The most significant human rights problems included abuses in the internal conflict, arbitrary or unlawful deprivation of life, and lack of respect for civil liberties.

Other human rights problems included: disappearances; potentially life-threatening prison and detention center conditions; restrictions on freedom of speech and press; arbitrary arrest or detention; restrictions on freedoms of assembly and association; arbitrary or unlawful interference with privacy; interference with participation in the political process; corruption and lack of transparency in government; restrictions on the rights of women, children, lesbian, gay, bisexual, transgender, and intersex (LGBTI) persons, and persons with disabilities; HIV and AIDS social stigma; societal violence against persons with albinism; restrictions on worker rights; and trafficking in persons.

The government took steps to investigate, prosecute, and punish some officials who committed abuses; however, impunity remained a problem at all levels.

Allegations surfaced in independent media of government-sponsored paramilitary "death squads" that targeted Renamo members. The government accused rebel forces belonging to Renamo of killing Frelimo officials, attacking civilian vehicles on major highways, and raiding numerous medical facilities. Renamo denied government and international nongovernmental organization (NGO) assertions that it attacked civilian vehicles, arguing it targeted FDS travelling in civilian vehicles wearing civilian attire. The government promised to investigate these actions; however, there were no prosecutions to date.

Section 1. Respect for the Integrity of the Person, Including Freedom from:

a. Arbitrary Deprivation of Life and other Unlawful or Politically Motivated Killings

There were numerous reports that the government or its agents committed arbitrary or unlawful killings. Most reports named security forces, particularly the National Police (PRM), as the perpetrators. The pattern of unidentified PRM officers killing unarmed civilians for minor infractions of the law (or sometimes no violation) continued throughout the country.

For example, in February an unidentified PRM officer in Beira shot and killed Cristovao Marcos Inoque, an auto rickshaw driver, because the officer thought Inoque was filming him drinking a beer on the job. In another incident local media reported unknown men, believed to be members of a government-sanctioned "death squad," abducted Gabriel Mateus, a local Renamo activist in Muxungue, Inhambane Province, on July 18. Residents found his body (which reportedly exhibited signs of torture) approximately two weeks later.

The high-profile 2015 killing of constitutional law professor Gilles Cistac remained unsolved. Cistac's death was widely considered politically motivated.

See section 1.g. for arbitrary or unlawful deprivation of life and other unlawful or politically motivated killings related to internal conflict.

b. Disappearance

There were several reports of politically motivated disappearances due to the internal conflict (see section 1.g.).

c. Torture and Other Cruel, Inhuman, or Degrading Treatment or Punishment

The constitution and law prohibit such practices; however, there were credible allegations of torture during the year (see Prison and Detention Center Conditions below and section 1.g.).

Prison and Detention Center Conditions

Some prisons in and around Maputo generally met international standards; however, prison conditions remained harsh and potentially life threatening in most areas due to gross overcrowding and inadequate sanitary conditions and medical care.

Physical Conditions: Government officials and civil society organizations continued to highlight overcrowding, juvenile prisoners in adult facilities, and convicted and untried prisoners sharing cells as serious problems. In September 2015 the national ombudsman called conditions in prisons and jails he visited in the northern city of Nampula "appalling." Local media reported in October 2015 that Maputo Central Prison held 2,500 prisoners despite its designed capacity for only 800.

The National Prisons Directorate's (SERNAP) director of health stated there were 51 deaths in all prisons in the first quarter of the year. Twenty-five of these prisoners died from HIV/AIDS, while 21 died of "other pathologies." SERNAP did not provide a cause of death for the remaining five. In April, SERNAP told local media that its statistics showed an estimated 20 percent of the approximately 15,000 prisoners were HIV-positive, compared with an estimated 11 percent of the country's total population.

Few prisons had health-care facilities or the ability to transport prisoners to outside facilities. Almost all prisons dated from the colonial era before 1975, leaving many in an advanced state of dilapidation. In April the Attorney General's Office (PGR) noted problems continued with the physical condition of prisons and overcrowding. In 2015 the PGR also noted problems with hygiene, food, medical assistance, and legal counseling.

Administration: In April prisoners at Mieze Open Provincial Penitentiary in Cabo Delgado Province accused certain guards of beating them with whips and dunking them in water tanks during a visit by the attorney general. The attorney general promised to investigate these allegations as well as allegations of prisoners being held in "preventive detention" beyond the legal maximum; however, the PGR did not release any findings. The LDH reported that record keeping improved compared with previous years. The PGR continued to note problems regarding prisoners held after completing their sentences or in excess of the maximum preventive detention period due to bureaucratic delays. No formal system specific to prisons existed for receiving or tracking complaints; however, prisoners were free to contact the PGR, national ombudsman, or NGOs with complaints.

Independent Monitoring: International and domestic human rights groups had access to prisoners at the discretion of the Ministry of Justice, Constitutional, and Religious Affairs and the Ministry of the Interior, and permission to visit prisoners was generally granted. The LDH and the National Commission on Human Rights (CNDH) had a high degree of access to prisons run by the Ministry of Justice due to written agreements. NGOs continued to have difficulty visiting detention facilities run by the Ministry of the Interior, particularly its detention facilities in police stations.

d. Arbitrary Arrest or Detention

The constitution and law prohibit arbitrary arrest and detention, and the government, with some exceptions, generally observed these prohibitions. Renamo accused government security forces of arbitrarily arresting its members multiple times. In one case, in February PRM officers broke into the house of Manuel Fortunato, a Renamo parliamentarian in the Sofala Provincial Assembly, in the middle of the night. They took him to the local police station for questioning regarding the attempted assassination of Renamo General Secretary Manuel Bissopo a month earlier. Inacio Dina, spokesperson for the PRM's General Command, later said "something went wrong" in Fortunato's detention.

Role of the Police and Security Apparatus

The Investigative Police (PIC), the PRM, and the Rapid Intervention Units (UIR) are responsible for internal security and report to the Ministry of the Interior. The Border Security Force also reports to the Interior Ministry and is responsible for protecting the country's international borders and for carrying out police duties within 24 miles of borders. An additional security body, the State Intelligence and Security Service, reports directly to the president and is responsible for intelligence operations. The Casa Militar (Presidential Guard) provides security for the president, and the Force for the Protection of High-Level Individuals provides security for other senior level officials at the national and provincial levels. The Mozambique Armed Defense Forces (FADM), consisting of the air force, army, and navy, are responsible for internal and external security and report to the Ministry of National Defense. The Estado Maior (General Staff) of the FADM plans all military operations. The president is commander in chief of the FADM. All of these forces are jointly referred to as the Defense and Security Forces.

Civilian authorities maintained control over the PIC, the PRM, UIR, and the Border Security Force with some exceptions; however, government mechanisms to investigate and punish abuse and corruption remained lacking. Multiple cases of arbitrary deprivation of life, disappearance, and arbitrary arrest demonstrated that impunity for perpetrators in the security forces remained widespread. Mozambican refugees who fled to Malawi in the first half of the year alleged abuses by security forces, including extrajudicial killings, beatings, rape, and destruction of property. Atanasio Mtumuke, the minister of defense, denied that security forces committed any abuses. The government pledged to investigate the allegations and make public its findings but did not release any report. It remained difficult to obtain information on security personnel accused of wrongdoing or any disciplinary or legal action taken against them. Police leadership acknowledged corruption was a problem.

Arrest Procedures and Treatment of Detainees

The law requires a judge or prosecutor to first issue an arrest warrant unless a person is caught in the act of committing a crime. By law the maximum length of investigative detention is 48 hours without a warrant or six months with a warrant, during which time a detainee has the right to judicial review of the case. An individual may be detained another 90 days while the PIC continues its investigation. A person accused of a crime carrying a potential maximum sentence of more than eight years may be detained up to an additional 84 days without being charged formally. A court may approve two more 84-day periods of detention without charge while police complete their investigation. The detainee must be released if no charges are brought within the prescribed period for investigation. Authorities generally did not detain individuals without judicial authorization. The law provides for citizens' right to access the courts and the right to legal representation, regardless of ability to pay for such services. Indigent defendants, however, frequently had no legal representation due to a shortage of legal professionals. There were no reports of suspects held incommunicado or under house arrest.

The bail system remained poorly defined.

Prisoners, their families, and NGOs complained prison officials demanded bribes to release prisoners who had already completed their sentences.

Pretrial Detention: Long pretrial detention continued to be a serious problem, due in part to an inadequate number of judges and prosecutors and poor communication among authorities. The PGR reported that 35 percent of prisoners nationwide were pretrial detainees in 2015, an increase from LDH's estimate of 31 percent in 2014. There were no reliable estimates of the average period of pretrial detention; however, some prisoners were held more than a year beyond the maximum investigative detention period.

Detainee's Ability to Challenge Lawfulness of Detention before a Court: Persons arrested or detained are entitled to challenge in court the legal basis or arbitrary nature of their detention and obtain prompt release if found to have been unlawfully detained. The law does not make any provisions for compensation in cases of unlawful detention. Many detainees were not able to take advantage of this right due to their inability to hire a lawyer and scarce resources for public defenders.

e. Denial of Fair Public Trial

The constitution and law provide for an independent judiciary; however, some civil society groups continued to assert the executive branch and ruling Frelimo party exerted influence on an understaffed and inadequately trained judiciary. In one case a provincial court convicted Saide Amido, the mayor of Lichinga, Niassa Province and a member of Frelimo, of corruption and abuse of power on May 24 and sentenced him to 18 months in jail. The court immediately converted the sentence into a 200,000 meticais ($2,790) fine. Amido returned to work on May

30. Comments on social media after his sentencing questioned the court's impartiality, given his political affiliation.

Trial Procedures

The constitution and law provide for the right to a fair and public trial without undue delay, and an independent judiciary generally enforced this right. Courts presume accused persons innocent, and the law provides the right to legal counsel and appeal. Defendants have the right to be informed promptly and in detail of the charges. Defendants have the right to be present at their trial. Defendants enjoy the right to communicate with an attorney of their choice, and the law specifically provides for public defenders for all defendants, although this did not always happen in practice. While defendants have adequate time to prepare a defense, they often did not have adequate facilities to do so.

By law only judges or lawyers may confront or question witnesses. A defendant may present witnesses and evidence on their own behalf and have access to government-held evidence. The government upheld such rights during the year. Defendants cannot be compelled to testify or confess guilt. Defendants also have the right to free interpretation as necessary from the moment charged through all appeals. The law extends the above rights to all defendants; the government did not deny any persons these rights.

Persons accused of crimes against the government, including treason or threatening national security, go to trial publicly in regular civilian courts under standard criminal judicial procedures. Members of the media and the general public attended trials throughout the year. A judge may order a trial closed to the media in the interest of national security, to protect the privacy of the plaintiff in a sexual assault case, or to prevent interested parties outside the court from destroying evidence.

Political Prisoners and Detainees

Unlike in previous years, there were no reports of political prisoners or detainees.

Civil Judicial Procedures and Remedies

While the law provides for an independent and impartial judiciary in civil matters, some citizens believed the judiciary was subject to political interference. Individuals or organizations may seek civil remedies for human rights violations through domestic courts. By law citizens have access to courts, the Office of the Ombudsperson, the CNDH, and the Bar Association to submit lawsuits seeking damages for, or cessation of, human rights violations. The country is a signatory to the Protocol to the African Charter on Human and Peoples' Rights on the Establishment of an African Court on Human and Peoples' Rights (the court); however, the country has not recognized the court's competency to receive cases from NGOs and individuals. In theory individuals and organizations can appeal adverse domestic decisions to the court.

f. Arbitrary or Unlawful Interference with Privacy, Family, Home, or Correspondence

The constitution and law prohibit such actions; however, there were reports the government at times failed to respect the privacy of personal communications. There were reports that government authorities entered homes without judicial or other appropriate authorization. Some civil society activists alleged government intelligence services and ruling party activists continued to monitor telephone calls and e-mails without warrants, conduct surveillance of their offices, follow opposition members, use informants, and disrupt opposition party activities in certain areas.

The Assembly of the Republic (parliament) passed legislation in March explicitly stating that a criminal investigation judge is the only legal authority who can authorize a wiretap. Many individuals reported the government unofficially required Frelimo party membership to obtain or retain government employment, obtain loans, and receive business licenses.

g. Abuses in Internal Conflict

Killings: The international NGO Human Rights Watch (HRW) criticized the government in February for multiple credible reports of unlawful killings in Tete Province that month, particularly in the village of Ndande. In August, LDH President Alice Mabota accused government forces of summarily executing "hundreds" during the year, although there was no evidence to support this allegation. The Portuguese news agency Lusa reported in March that villagers in the Gorongosa area of Sofala discovered a mass grave containing 120 bodies. The government said the report was "disinformation" and cordoned off the area around the alleged site, denying journalists and NGOs access to investigate Lusa's story. In May photojournalists and independent television station STV confirmed the presence of between 13 and 15 bodies near and under a bridge in Manica. A reported second mass gravesite was later found close by. While a parliamentary investigative team did not come to any definitive conclusions or hold the government responsible, it was the first time such an investigative committee was formed.

Independent media and Renamo claimed the government operated "death squads" to kill specific Renamo members. For example, unidentified gunmen fatally shot Jose Manuel, a senior Renamo official and member of the National Defense and Security Council. The government denied the existence of death squads and promised to investigate the allegations.

A pattern of reprisal killings between Renamo and government forces occurred throughout the year. For example, in May Renamo gunmen killed two civilians and injured eight in an attack on a private bus on the main highway in the Honde area of Manica Province. Renamo denied targeting civilians and claimed it only targeted government security forces allegedly wearing civilian attire and travelling in civilian vehicles.

After months of clashes, in July peace talks between the government and Renamo commenced; they were suspended in August, without achieving a ceasefire, and restarted in September.

Abductions: Deutsche Welle reported in June that security forces in the village of Mucodza, Sofala Province, kidnapped several men and demanded that they show them the location of Renamo bases in the area and identify Renamo militants. The men said they did not know anything about Renamo locations. Security forces shot one of the men as he attempted to flee.

Physical Abuse, Punishment, and Torture: There were multiple accusations of rape and sexual assault by government forces from women who fled Tete Province. There were also allegations of physical abuse by those who fled to Malawi. Amnesty International reported in May that three men dressed in civilian clothes abducted Benedito Sabao, a farmer in Manica Province, and took him to the Cantandica District Command police station. The men, believed by Amnesty International to belong to the State Information and Security Service, asked Sabao to reveal the whereabouts of local Renamo members. Sabao denied knowing any Renamo members and said the police station commander and the local head of the PIC pistol-whipped and beat him. Sabao said the men who abducted him later took him to a field and shot him; he survived.

<u>Other Conflict-related Abuse</u>: LDH President Alice Mabota termed the conflict "a low intensity civil war." More than 10,000 citizens fled Tete Province for neighboring Malawi in the first six months of the year. Authorities denied for months that any refugees had fled the country. When they acknowledged that some persons fled, government officials claimed they did so because of food insecurity or Renamo attacks. Many told NGOs they were fleeing abuses by government forces. The LDH and HRW reported during the year security forces burned the houses of suspected Renamo sympathizers while searching for combatants. The government sent a delegation to investigate that has not released any findings; however, a Freedom House report released in December documented refugee claims that they were fleeing abuse by government soldiers.

In August, HRW criticized Renamo for attacking at least two hospitals and health clinics in Zambezia Province during the month. HRW said the attacks interrupted health-care access to thousands in remote areas of the province. Subsequently HRW publicly called on the South African Development Community to "intervene" in Mozambique, citing the attacks on health-care facilities as an escalation of the conflict. On multiple occasions throughout the year, Renamo forces attacked civilian vehicles on highways in central provinces with small arms, claiming the vehicles were carrying government soldiers or military supplies. The attacks killed several and injured dozens of persons over the course of the year.

Section 2. Respect for Civil Liberties, Including:

a. Freedom of Speech and Press

The constitution and law provide for freedom of speech and press, and the government generally respected this right; however, the government did not always effectively protect nor respect these freedoms. Academics, journalists, opposition party officials, and civil society reported an atmosphere of intimidation and fear that continued to restrict freedom of speech and press. Allegations included the use of threatening messages via text and Facebook, physical confrontations, and widely circulated "WhatsApp" messages targeting anyone critical of the government. The abduction and shooting of independent journalist Jose Jaime Macuane (see Violence and Harassment) caused particular concern.

<u>Freedom of Speech and Expression</u>: There were no official restrictions on the ability of individuals to criticize the government or restriction on the discussion of matters of general public interest; however, police imposed de facto restrictions on free speech and expression throughout the year. Opposition and civil society

complained they could not freely criticize the government without fear of reprisal, particularly since the March 2015 murder of prominent jurist Gilles Cistac remained unsolved. Multiple civil society figures, including LDH President Mabota, received anonymous threatening text messages after criticizing the government. One academic said the local head of Frelimo visited his mother and threatened her. At least one academic temporarily left the country after receiving such messages.

On March 18, PRM officials arrested Eva Anadon Moreno, a Spanish citizen who worked with various women's empowerment groups and had lived in the country for six years, for her part in a "street action" organized by women's rights umbrella group Forum Mulher (Women's Forum). The protest was intended to draw attention to gender-based violence in schools across the country. The PRM released Anadon several hours after her arrest. Immigration officials later visited her at her apartment the night of March 29 and asked her to accompany them to their headquarters. Instead, they took her to Maputo's international airport where they detained her overnight. Immigration officials deported Anadon on a commercial flight to South Africa the following day. She did not receive a hearing or a chance to appeal her deportation.

<u>Press and Media Freedoms</u>: The government exerted substantial pressure on all forms of media. The NGO Selekani reported that media outlets and journalists frequently self-censored to avoid government retaliation. In May, Isaque Chande, the minister of justice, constitutional, and religious affairs, threatened to trigger "accountability mechanisms" against the Portuguese news agency Lusa for publishing local residents' allegations of a mass grave containing 120 bodies in Sofala Province. The government denied the existence of any mass graves, and security forces kept journalists away from the alleged location.

<u>Violence and Harassment</u>: In May unidentified gunmen posing as police officers abducted journalist Jose Jaime Macuane outside his home in Maputo and drove him to a rural area in Maputo Province. They told him they had orders to cripple him and shot him four times in the legs. Macuane was a cohost of the political talk show *Pontos de vista* ("Points of View") on STV, an independent television station. Local media speculated that he was targeted for criticizing the government. In response to the shooting, Tomas Viera Mario, chair of the country's Higher Mass Media Council, said journalists were "facing a serious assault against human rights." The government did not criticize the shooting.

In June, PIC officers questioned Joao Chamusse and Egidio Placido, manager and editor in chief, respectively, of the print weekly newspaper *Zambeze*, for several hours regarding their sources after they published an article. The article claimed that Renamo fighters killed an unknown number of Zimbabwean soldiers who were on a combat mission in the central part of the country.

<u>Censorship or Content Restrictions</u>: There were no official government guidelines for media. Media officials reported the government's Information Office convened regular editorial board meetings to coordinate and direct news content released by state-controlled media. Some journalists reported pressure to self-censor. Some media officials stated critical reporting could result in cancellation of government and ruling party advertising contracts. The largest advertising revenue streams for local media came from ministries and state-controlled businesses. Selekani noted the government asserted its control over state-owned media by giving media outlets their annual budgets in small increments, with the amounts determined by how faithfully articles hewed to official positions.

Internet Freedom

The government did not restrict access to the internet or censor online content. Members of civil society reported government intelligence agents monitored e-mail and used false names to infiltrate social network discussion groups. Local internet freedom advocates believed the intelligence service monitored online content critical of the government. Government officials expressed interest in discovering the identity of "Unay Cambuma," a pro-Renamo person or group that published Facebook posts critical of the government and that appeared to have intimate knowledge of government operations.

According to the World Bank, 6 percent of persons in the country used the internet during the year.

Academic Freedom and Cultural Events

There were no government restrictions on academic freedom or cultural events; however, certain academics reported self-censorship. Despite the law providing for separation of party and state, primary school teachers in Gaza Province reportedly included Frelimo party propaganda in their curriculum.

b. Freedom of Peaceful Assembly and Association

Freedom of Assembly

The constitution and law provide for freedom of assembly; nevertheless, the government did not always respect this right. By law protest organizers do not require government "authorization" to peacefully protest; however, protest organizers must notify local authorities of their intent in writing at least four business days beforehand. The government used alleged errors in protest organizers' notification documents to disallow protests. For example, on May 14, organizations sent Maputo Mayor David Simango a letter to notify their intent to organize a march against recently revealed (109 billion meticais) $1.5 billion in "hidden" sovereign guarantees for loans to state-owned enterprises contracted by the previous administration. Simango replied that the march could not take place as planned since he could not determine if the letter's signatories represented the organizations they claimed to. Unknown assailants abducted and beat Joao Massango, protest spokesperson and president of the Earth Ecologists Movement Party, shortly after the Mayor's Office received the notification.

Freedom of Association

The constitution and law provide for freedom of association, and the government generally respected this right. The Ministry of Justice, Constitutional, and Religious Affairs did not act on LAMBDA's (the country's only LGBTI advocacy NGO) registration request, which was pending since 2008. The registration process usually takes less than two months. Civil society leaders and some diplomatic missions continued to urge Justice Minister Chande to act on LAMBDA's application and to treat all registration applications fairly. Minister Chande and other government officials cited the country's culture and religious sentiments as reasons the ministry had not acted.

c. Freedom of Religion

See the Department of State's *International Religious Freedom Report* at www.state.gov/religiousfreedomreport/.

d. Freedom of Movement, Internally Displaced Persons, Protection of Refugees, and Stateless Persons

The constitution and law provide for freedom of internal movement, foreign travel, emigration, and repatriation, and the government generally respected these rights.

<u>Abuse of Migrants, Refugees, and Stateless Persons</u>: The government generally cooperated with the Office of the United Nations High Commissioner for Refugees (UNHCR) and other humanitarian organizations in providing protection and assistance to refugees, asylum seekers, stateless persons, and other persons of concern. There were exceptions: for example, in April local authorities arbitrarily arrested and detained a Congolese refugee living at the Maratane refugee camp in Nampula. Officials accused him of involvement in the vandalism of a health center in September 2015 despite the fact he was nowhere near the health center at the time. Authorities eventually released him.

<u>In-country Movement</u>: In February the government introduced convoys with armed police escorts on three stretches of highway in Sofala and Manica to protect civilian vehicles from Renamo attacks. Renamo ambushes on civilian vehicles in Manica, Sofala, and Zambezia significantly diminished persons' ability to move freely throughout the country. In March several bus companies in Nampula announced they were cancelling service to Maputo due to the attacks.

Refugees must formally request authorization to move outside the geographic region of their registration. The government usually authorized these requests, with the exception of requests to move to the city of Maputo.

Internally Displaced Persons

By law only persons in an official internally displaced persons (IDPs) camp are considered internally displaced. In August, Lusa reported that the National Institute for Disaster Management (INGC) recognized 2,372 IDPs and established camps for persons fleeing food insecurity due to drought in Manica. INGC Director for Prevention and Migration Ana Christina acknowledged that some of the IDPs in these camps fled the conflict between the government and Renamo. Additionally, Deutsche Welle reported in June that more than 500 families who fled the village of Pembe (Inhambane Province) in January 2014 due to fighting between government forces and Renamo remained internally displaced. The local government created a resettlement area approximately 16 miles away to house the families.

Protection of Refugees

<u>Access to Asylum</u>: The law provides for the granting of asylum or refugee status, and the government has established a system for providing protection to refugees. The government provided protection against the expulsion or return of refugees to

countries where their lives or freedom would be threatened on account of their race, religion, nationality, membership in a particular social group, or political opinion.

Durable Solutions: The government continued to work closely with UNHCR to implement a local integration program for refugees at the Maratane Camp in Nampula Province. UNHCR referred a limited number of refugees for third country resettlement.

Section 3. Freedom to Participate in the Political Process

The constitution and law provide citizens the ability to choose their government in free and fair periodic elections held by secret ballot and based on universal and equal suffrage.

Elections and Political Participation

Recent Elections: Domestic and international observers noted voting-day procedures during the most recent presidential and national legislative elections in October 2014 were generally orderly but lacked transparency during vote tabulation. Some domestic and foreign observers and local civil society organizations criticized irregularities, including delays in observer credentialing, excessive numbers of invalid votes, and inordinately high voter turnout in some districts, which they alleged indicated ballot box stuffing. Renamo did not recognize the election results as legitimate, and Renamo officials initially refused to take their seats in parliament and the provincial assemblies but ended their boycott in February 2015. Frelimo and the Mozambican Democratic Movement (MDM) accepted the results.

During the campaign period, representatives of opposition parties and civil society complained of increased acts of bias and intimidation by the government and Frelimo. For example, in June 2014 election officials in Cabo Delgado Province held local meetings excluding the newly designated Renamo members, alleging a lack of meeting space. Independent reporting corroborated opposition parties' accusations that Frelimo used state funds and resources for campaign purposes in violation of electoral law. Renamo sought to justify its use of violence by citing alleged fraud in the 2014 elections.

Political Parties and Political Participation: Frelimo continued to dominate the political process as it had throughout the 41 years since independence. Opposition political parties could operate, yet there continued to be occasional restrictions on meetings, unlawful arrests, and other forms of interference and harassment by the government. MDM, the second largest opposition party, won four key mayoral seats in the 2013 municipal elections and seven seats in the 2014 parliamentary elections, but it won only 7 percent of the popular vote in the 2014 presidential contest. Media bias in state-owned outlets in favor of Frelimo continued. The EU election observation mission criticized state-owned or affiliated media bias in its 2014 election report.

Security forces and private citizens continued to harass opposition party members. In one instance Renamo told local media the PRM prevented its members from holding a meeting at a Maputo hotel. According to Renamo, the PRM ordered the hotel to cancel the event, and there was a large police presence when Renamo members arrived. Inacio Dina, PRM general command spokesperson, said the PRM officers were there to ensure safety. There were also reports of three arson attacks against Renamo provincial headquarters in Chimoio, capital of Manica Province.

Participation of Women and Minorities: No laws, cultural practices, or traditions prevent women or members of minorities from voting, running for office, serving as electoral monitors, or otherwise participating in political life. Women and members of many ethnic groups held key political positions.

Section 4. Corruption and Lack of Transparency in Government

The law provides criminal penalties for corrupt acts by officials; however, the government did not implement the law effectively, and officials often engaged in corrupt practices with impunity. Corruption continued to be a problem in all branches of government and at all levels.

Corruption: Corruption, including extortion by police, remained widespread, and impunity remained a serious problem. Police regularly demanded identification documents or cited alleged vehicular infractions solely to extort bribes. High-level corruption continued to affect the country. The Center for Public Integrity (CIP) released a study in May that estimated corruption had cost the state up to 378 billion meticais ($5.3 billion) over the past 10 years.

Negative fiscal ramifications from the 2013 EMATUM (a state-owned tuna fishing company) transaction, which directly related to lack of transparency in the public tender process, continued during the year. Additionally, Adriano Maleiane, minister of finance and the economy, publicly announced in April that two companies, Proindicus and Mozambique Assets Management, had contracted previously undisclosed debts worth nearly 109 billion meticais ($1.5 billion) for which the government provided sovereign guarantees. The International Monetary Fund (IMF) and international donors demanded an independent, international audit of the loan and the disposition of the borrowed funds. The government promised a thorough internal review led by the PGR. The government agreed to conduct an audit under IMF-defined terms of reference. The PGR stated it continued to conduct its review.

Financial Disclosure: The law requires annual income and assets disclosure by appointed and elected members of the government and high-ranking civil servants to the Ministry of State Administration. The law provides for fines for those who do not file declarations; however, the declarations are not public. In January, CIP said the process of requiring public servants to file financial disclosures was "still not effective."

Public Access to Information: The government continued to struggle to implement the Freedom of Information Act of 2014. A report issued in May by two media-focused NGOs contacted 49 public entities to request information and found that only 18 percent responded within 21 days as required by law.

Section 5. Governmental Attitude Regarding International and Nongovernmental Investigation of Alleged Violations of Human Rights

A number of domestic and international human rights groups generally operated without government restriction, investigating and publishing their findings on human rights cases. Government officials were somewhat cooperative and responsive to their views. The government did not act on the registration request of a local LGBTI organization. The government frequently denied or delayed NGOs' access to areas where abuses by security forces allegedly occurred. Security forces kept NGOs from investigating the location in Sofala where Lusa reported local residents alleged they found a mass grave.

Government Human Rights Bodies: The CNDH is mandated to promote and defend human rights by ensuring that the human rights provisions of the constitution are followed. Its stated priorities are cases of law enforcement violence, judicial corruption, and violations of prisoner rights. The commission lacks authority to prosecute violations and must refer cases to the judiciary. The commission members are chosen by the political parties, civil society, the prime minister, and the Mozambican Bar Association choose CNDH members. It received funding from foreign donors and the UN Development Program.

Section 6. Discrimination, Societal Abuses, and Trafficking in Persons

Women

<u>Rape and Domestic Violence</u>: The law criminalizes rape, including spousal rape, and domestic violence. Penalties range from two to eight years' imprisonment if the victim is 12 years of age or older and 20 to 24 years' imprisonment if the victim is under 12. Civil society organizations noted that while the wording of the revised penal code, passed in 2014, covers both vaginal and anal sex, it does not cover other forms of rape such as oral sex and insertion of objects. Legal experts also noted the definition of "intercourse" in the new penal code meant that men could also qualify as victims of rape. The penal code does not allow victims to drop charges for rape when they marry the perpetrator.

According to NGO reports, many families preferred to settle rape allegations through informal community courts or privately through financial remuneration rather than through the formal judicial system. Cases of spousal rape continued to be underreported. Increasing numbers of victims continued to seek assistance from human rights organizations, especially in cases that resulted in HIV infection.

Abuse of a spouse or unmarried partner is punishable with one to two years in prison, or a greater penalty if another crime is also applicable. The government did not effectively enforce the law. NGOs reported that domestic violence against women remained widespread. Maria Luisa, spokeswoman for the Mozambican Association Women, Law, and Development, said cases of domestic violence were rising at a "frightening" level.

Although domestic violence was considered a valid reason to leave a partner, women often had few economic or social alternatives and thus remained with the abuser since many were dependent on the community or family-based (typically agricultural) economy. Many young women also engaged in transactional sex with older, wealthier men in order to survive economically.

With the exception of some ethnic and religious groups, the groom's family provided a bride price to the bride's family, usually in the form of money, livestock, or other goods, although this practice had become somewhat less common. Some believed these payments contributed to violence against women and other inequalities due to the perception that husbands owned and paid for their wives. Among Muslims, the bride's family usually paid for the wedding and provided gifts.

Government agencies and NGOs continued to implement public outreach campaigns to combat violence against women nationwide. Police and NGOs worked together to combat domestic violence. The PRM operated special women's and children's units within police precincts that received high numbers of cases of domestic violence, sexual assault, and violence against children.

Female Genital Mutilation/Cutting (FGM/C): FGM/C was not a common practice for women or girls in the country. Reliable estimates were lacking on the number of women subjected to FGM/C in recent years; however, NGOs and the government concurred that the incidence was low.

Other Harmful Traditional Practices: The practice of "purification," whereby a widow is obligated to have unprotected sex with a member of her deceased husband's family, continued, particularly in rural areas, despite campaigns against it.

Sexual Harassment: Sexual harassment is illegal in schools; however, it remained pervasive in business, government, schools, and broadly in society. There is no legislation on sexual harassment in public places outside of schools.

Reproductive Rights: Couples and individuals have the right to decide the number, spacing, and timing of their children; manage their reproductive health; and have access to the information and means to do so, free from discrimination, coercion, and violence. Health-care clinics and local NGOs operated freely and disseminated information on family planning; however, only 12 percent (down from 17 percent in 2004) of girls and women ages 15-49 used modern contraception, according to the World Bank. Rural communities often had limited access to basic health services. Many people in poor communities believed large families enhanced wealth generation.

The country had a maternal mortality rate of 489 deaths per 100,000 live births in 2015, and a woman's lifetime risk of maternal death was one in 40, according to the UN Population Fund, due in part to poor clinical capacity for obstetric emergencies and a severe lack of doctors (approximately 3,000 for an estimated population of 25 million in 2015) and nurses, particularly in rural areas. Other reasons included poor infrastructure, a high HIV/AIDS rate, high rates of adolescent pregnancy, and poor access to health-care facilities, often resulting in delays in providing medical care.

Discrimination: The law provides the same legal status and rights for women as men; however, it does not specifically require equal pay for equal work, nor does it prohibit discrimination based on gender in hiring. The law also contains provisions that limit excessive physical work or night shift requirements during pregnancy. The law contains special provisions to protect women against abuse; however, many women remained uninformed about the law.

Women continued to experience economic discrimination. Relative gender gaps in education and income remained high. In some regions, particularly the northern provinces, women had limited access to the formal judicial system for enforcement of rights provided under the civil code and instead relied on customary law to settle disputes. Women typically have no rights to inherit land under customary law, leaving women in rural areas particularly vulnerable to property rights discrimination.

Women held a relatively small proportion of private-sector salaried jobs, and they had correspondingly lower social security benefits. Many worked as casual laborers or elsewhere in the informal sector, primarily in subsistence agriculture. Enforcement of laws that protect women's rights to land ownership remained poor. Forum Mulher continued to note that women's representation in local and provincial-level bodies continued to lag, while their representation in national decision-making bodies was relatively high.

The parliament has a women's caucus, composed of members from the three parties with parliamentary seats, which seeks to address issues of gender balance, women's representation in decision-making bodies, and advocacy of women's rights.

Children

Birth Registration: Citizenship is obtained by birth in the country or birth to at least one Mozambican parent outside the country. Failure to register a child's birth may result in the inability to attend school and may prevent one from obtaining public documents, such as identity cards, passports, or "poverty certificates," which enable access to free health care and free secondary education. Birth registration was often delayed in rural areas. Cultural practices continued to deprive women, especially in rural areas, of their legal right to register their child without the presence of the child's father.

Education: Although education is compulsory through primary school (grades one to seven), primary school completion remained beyond the means of many families, especially in rural areas. Families must pay for supplies and uniforms despite the fact that school is tuition-free and compulsory through grade seven. According to the government's 2010 Millennium Development Goals report, despite joint government-NGO initiatives in some localities to improve girls' school attendance, only 27 percent of girls finished primary school, compared with 40 percent of boys.

Child Abuse: Most child-abuse cases involved sexual or physical abuse. Sexual abuse in schools and in homes continued to be a problem. NGOs remained concerned that certain male teachers used their authority to coerce female students into sex. A UNESCO policy paper published in March 2015 noted approximately 20 percent of school principals said sexual harassment of students by teachers or other pupils occurred at least "sometimes" at their schools.

While the government continued to stress the importance of children's rights and welfare, significant problems remained. The child protection law contains sections dealing with protection against physical and sexual abuse; removal from parents who are unable to protect, assist, and educate them; and the establishment of juvenile courts to deal with matters of adoption, maintenance, and regulating parental power. Juvenile courts resolved many cases regarding support for children after divorce or the end of a relationship.

Orphans and other vulnerable children remained at high risk of abuse.

Early and Forced Marriage: The law sets the minimum age to marry for both genders at 18. Legal permission to marry at age 16 may be granted with parental consent if "circumstances of recognized public and family interest," such as pregnancy, exist. According to a 2015 UNICEF report, nationwide 48 percent of young women ages 20-24 married before age 18, and 14 percent of women ages 20-24 married before age 15. The highest rates of early marriage were in the northern provinces of Cabo Delgado and Nampula, where 61 percent and 62 percent of women were married before age 18, respectively. In Niassa, another northern province, 24 percent of young women married before age 15, the highest rate in the country. The government and local NGOs continued to campaign against child marriage.

<u>Female Genital Mutilation/Cutting (FGM/C)</u>: See Female Genital Mutilation/Cutting (FGM/C) under Women.

<u>Sexual Exploitation of Children</u>: The law prohibits the commercial sexual exploitation of children and child pornography. Authorities partially enforced the law, but exploitation of children below age 18 and child prostitution remained problematic. The minimum age for consensual sex is 16. Underage girls were exploited in prostitution in bars, roadside clubs, and restaurants. Child prostitution appeared to be most prevalent in Maputo, Nampula, Beira, border towns, and at overnight stopping points along key transportation routes. Some NGOs provided health care, counseling, and vocational training to children, primarily girls, engaged in prostitution.

<u>Displaced Children</u>: Children from Zimbabwe, Malawi, and Swaziland, many of whom had entered the country alone, remained vulnerable to labor exploitation and discrimination. They lacked protection due to inadequate documentation and had limited access to schools and other social welfare institutions, largely due to lack of resources. Coercion, both physical and economic, of girls into the sex industry was common, particularly in Manica Province.

Child beggars and children selling snacks, who appeared to be living on the streets, remained visible in major urban areas, but no nationwide figures were available. NGOs said many lived in crowded housing with their "bosses" and came from poorer areas in the north.

Several government agencies, including the Ministry of Health and the Ministry of Gender, Children, and Social Action, continued programs to provide health-care assistance and vocational education for HIV/AIDS orphans and other vulnerable children.

<u>International Child Abductions</u>: The country is not a party to the 1980 Hague Convention on the Civil Aspects of International Child Abduction. See the Department of State's *Annual Report on International Parental Child Abduction* at <u>travel.state.gov/content/childabduction/en/legal/compliance.html</u>.

Anti-Semitism

The country has a very small Jewish community. There were no reports of anti-Semitic acts.

Trafficking in Persons

See the Department of State's *Trafficking in Persons Report* at
www.state.gov/j/tip/rls/tiprpt/.

Persons with Disabilities

The constitution and law prohibit discrimination against citizens with disabilities;
however, the law does not differentiate between physical, sensory, intellectual, and
mental disabilities in employment, education, air travel and other transportation,
access to health care, the judicial system, or the provision of other state services.

The Ministry of Gender, Children, and Social Action is responsible for protecting
the rights of persons with disabilities. The 2012-19 National Action Plan in the
Area of Disabilities provides funding, monitoring, and assessment of
implementation by various organizations that support persons with disabilities.
Electoral law provides for access and assistance to voters with disabilities in the
polling booths, including the right for them to vote first.

The government did not effectively implement laws and programs to provide
access to buildings, information, and communications. Discrimination in
employment, education, access to health care, and the provision of other state
services was common. Observers often cited unequal access to employment as one
of the biggest concerns. The government did not effectively implement programs
to provide access to information and communication for persons with disabilities.
Educational opportunities for children with disabilities were generally poor,
especially for those with developmental disabilities. The government sometimes
referred parents of children with disabilities to private schools with more resources
to provide for their children. There were two schools for persons with disabilities:
one in Maputo Province and one in Sofala. The Mozambican Association for the
Disabled (ADEMO) reported teacher-training programs did not include techniques
on how to address the needs of students with disabilities. ADEMO also observed
school buildings fell short of international standards for accessibility, and public
tenders were not designed to support the participation of persons with disabilities.

The only psychiatric hospital was overwhelmed with patients and did not provide
adequate basic nutrition, medicine, or shelter. Doctors also reported many families
abandoned family members with disabilities at the hospital. ADEMO reported

access to donated equipment, such as wheelchairs, continued to be a challenge due to lengthy and complicated bureaucratic procedures.

The city of Maputo offered free bus passes to persons with disabilities. Buses in Maputo did not have specific accessibility features. Because public transportation was limited, many citizens rode in private minibuses and in the backs of pickup trucks, hazardous for persons with or without disabilities. Access ramps were rare, and sidewalks were hazardous for pedestrians to traverse.

Acts of Violence, Discrimination, and Other Abuses Based on Sexual Orientation and Gender Identity

There were reports of societal discrimination based on sexual orientation and gender identity. Antidiscrimination laws protected LGBTI persons only from employment discrimination. No hate crime laws or other criminal justice mechanisms exist to aid in the prosecution of bias-motivated crimes against LGBTI persons. The government took no action on the only LGBTI association's 2008 request to register legally.

The government does not track or report discrimination or crimes against individuals based on sexual orientation or gender identity. LAMBDA and local media did not report any bias-based attacks; however, discrimination in public medical facilities continued to occur. Medical staff sometimes chastised LGBTI individuals for their sexual orientation upon seeking treatment. Intimidation was not a factor in preventing incidents of abuse from being reported.

HIV and AIDS Social Stigma

The Joint UN Program on HIV and AIDS (UNAIDS) estimated that 11 percent of the population between the ages of 15 and 49 lived with HIV or AIDS in 2015. In August a government spokesperson stated the country registered approximately 107 AIDS-related deaths in addition to 223 new HIV infections daily. UNAIDS reported that in 2015, 28 percent of the population held "discriminatory attitudes" towards persons living with HIV or AIDS.

According to the 2013 People Living with HIV Stigma Index, 24 percent of respondents were verbally threatened or insulted, 20 percent excluded from family or social events, and 5 percent physically assaulted due to their HIV status. Reports continued of many women expelled from their homes and abandoned by their husbands and relatives because they were HIV-positive. Family or community members accused some women widowed by HIV/AIDS of being witches who purposely killed their husbands to acquire belongings; as retribution, they deprived the women of all possessions.

Other Societal Violence or Discrimination

Albimoz and Amor a Vida, local NGOs that advocated for persons with albinism, continued to document cases in which assailants kidnapped, maimed, or killed persons with albinism. Criminals attacked persons with albinism, often with the assistance of a family member, because certain witch doctors, purportedly from outside the country, according to government officials, paid for their body parts due to their allegedly "magical" properties. For example, in June criminals in Manica Province kidnapped and dismembered a six-year-old child with albinism.

The government continued to denounce violence against persons with albinism. Local media reported that police in Nampula had arrested 50 individuals suspected of kidnapping and murdering persons with albinism between January 2015 and May 2016. Courts tended to sentence those convicted of the murder and/or kidnapping of persons with albinism more harshly than those convicted of similar crimes that did not involve persons with albinism.

Section 7. Worker Rights

a. Freedom of Association and the Right to Collective Bargaining

The constitution and law provide that workers, with limited exceptions, may form and join independent trade unions, conduct legal strikes, and bargain collectively. The law requires government approval to establish a union. The government has 45 days to register an employers' or workers' organization, a delay the International Labor Organization (ILO) deemed excessive. Although the law provides for the right of workers to organize and engage in collective bargaining, such contracts covered less than 5 percent of the workforce. Workers in defense and security services, tax administration, prison workers, the fire brigade, judges and prosecutors, and the President's Office staff members are prohibited from unionizing. Other public-sector workers may form and join unions, but they are prohibited from striking.

The law does not allow strike action until complex conciliation, mediation, and arbitration procedures have been exhausted, which typically takes two to three weeks. Sectors deemed essential must provide a "minimum level" of service during a strike. Workers' ability to conduct union activities in workplaces was strictly limited. The law provides for voluntary arbitration for "essential services" personnel monitoring the weather and fuel supply, postal service workers, export processing zone (EPZ) workers, and those loading and unloading animals and perishable foodstuffs. Strikes must be announced at least five days in advance, and the announcement must include the expected duration of the strike, although the government interprets this to allow indefinite strikes. Mediation and arbitration bodies can end strikes in addition to the unions and workers themselves. The law prohibits all types of antiunion discrimination; however, it does not explicitly provide for reinstatement of workers terminated for union activities.

Authorities and employers generally respected freedom of association and the right to collective bargaining, although workers exercised few of these rights. There are strict legal constraints on workers' meetings in the workplace. While unions occasionally negotiated wage increases and organized strikes, such activities were infrequent. The government also respected the legal prohibition of antiunion discrimination. There were no reports of violations related to freedom of association and collective bargaining rights or antiunion discrimination during the year.

A lack of resources continued to hamper the government's efforts to enforce many of its labor laws. Government efforts included fining companies that violated labor laws and the expulsion of foreign supervisors who allegedly did not follow the law. Fines were not sufficient to deter violators.

The International Trade Union Confederation criticized the government's prohibition of strikes by EPZ workers and claimed they do not meet the ILO's definition of "essential services" workers. The ILO had previously criticized the government's definition of "essential services" workers as being too broad.

The largest trade union organization, OTM-Central Sindical (Mozambican Worker's Organization-Central Syndicate), was perceived as biased in favor of the government and ruling party Frelimo.

b. Prohibition of Forced or Compulsory Labor

The law prohibits all forms of forced or compulsory labor. The law against trafficking in persons, which includes forced labor, prescribes penalties of 16 to 20 years' imprisonment for human traffickers.

The government continued to have difficulties enforcing these laws effectively. There was limited evidence of forced labor and forced child labor in the domestic and agricultural sectors. Women and girls from rural areas, as well as migrant workers from bordering countries, were lured to cities with false promises of employment or education and then were exploited in domestic servitude and sex trafficking.

Also see the Department of State's *Trafficking in Persons Report* at www.state.gov/j/tip/rls/tiprpt/.

c. Prohibition of Child Labor and Minimum Age for Employment

The minimum working age without restrictions is 18. The law permits children between the ages of 15 and 17 to work with a Ministry of Labor permit. The employer is required to provide for their education and training and provide conditions of work that are not damaging to their physical and moral development. Children between the ages of 12 and 14 may work under special conditions authorized by the Ministries of Labor, Health, and Education. Children under 18 may work up to seven hours a day for a total of 38 hours a week. They are not permitted to work in occupations that are unhealthy, dangerous, or require significant physical effort; however, the government has no official list of prohibited job activities or occupations. By law children must be paid at least the minimum wage or a minimum of two-thirds of the adult salary, whichever is higher. Labor inspectors may obtain court orders and use police to enforce compliance with child labor provisions.

The Ministry of Labor regulates child labor in the formal sector, but the government did not effectively enforce the law. There were no mechanisms in place for submitting complaints about hazardous and forced child labor. Violations of child labor provisions are punishable with fines ranging from one to 40 months of the minimum wage. Such penalties were insufficient to deter violations. Enforcement mechanisms generally were inadequate in the formal sector due to resource constraints and nonexistent in the informal sector.

The labor inspectorate and police lacked adequate staff, funds, and training to investigate child labor cases, especially in areas outside the capital, where a majority of the abuses occurred. No labor inspectors specialized in child labor issues; however, they all received child labor training. Inspectors earned low wages (like many government employees) making them vulnerable to, and often inclined to seek, bribes. Inspectors often did not have the means to travel to sites and therefore relied on the company they were investigating to provide transportation to the site of an alleged violation. Although the government provided training for police on child prostitution and abuse prevention, there was no specialized child labor training for the police.

Child labor remained a problem. NGOs reported some girls from rural areas migrated to urban centers to work as domestic help for extended family or acquaintances to settle debts where they were vulnerable to commercial sexual exploitation (see section 6, Children). Mothers who did not complete secondary school were more likely to have children involved in child labor. Due to economic necessity, especially in rural areas, children worked in agriculture, as domestic employees, or in prostitution.

Children, including those under age 15, commonly worked on family farms harvesting rice, cotton, tobacco, or tea. They were often paid on a piecework basis rather than an hourly minimum wage. NGOs indicated that in the northern provinces of Zambezia, Nampula, and Cabo Delgado, adults hired to work on tobacco, cotton, and cashew plantations routinely had their children also work to increase family income. These children worked long hours and were prevented from attending school.

Also see the Department of Labor's *Findings on the Worst Forms of Child Labor* at www.dol.gov/ilab/reports/child-labor/findings/.

d. Discrimination with Respect to Employment and Occupation

The law prohibits discrimination with respect to employment and occupation based on race, color, sex, religion, political opinion, national origin, citizenship, social origin, disability, sexual orientation, gender identity, age, language, and HIV-positive status or having other communicable diseases.

The law explicitly prohibits discrimination against workers because of HIV/AIDS status, and the Ministry of Labor generally intervened in cases of perceived discrimination by employers. With an increased public awareness of this law, there were no public reports of individuals dismissed because of their HIV status.

The government effectively enforced applicable law. Penalties (such as fines) were sufficient to deter violations.

There were multiple reports in local media of the Labor Ministry suspending the contracts of irregular foreign workers. Some foreign workers reported harassment by Labor Ministry inspectors after disputes with Mozambican coworkers and being forced to pay bribes for work permits or leave the country.

e. Acceptable Conditions of Work

The lowest government-mandated industry-based minimum wage was 3,183 meticais ($44) a month and can be adjusted as needed. The poverty line was 540 meticais ($7.50) per member of household a month. Workers generally received benefits, such as transportation and food, in addition to wages. The OTM estimated that a minimum livable monthly wage to provide for a family of five was 8,000 meticais ($111). The standard legal workweek is 40 hours but may be extended to 48 hours. Overtime must be paid over 48 hours at 50 percent above the base hourly salary. The law limits overtime to two hours per day and 100 hours per year. The law provides for one hour of rest per workday. Foreign workers are protected under the law but must apply for work permits. Health and environmental laws were in place to protect workers in the formal sector; however, the informal economy comprised an estimated 95 percent of the workforce.

The government sets occupational health and safety (OSH) standards that are current and appropriate for the main industries. Workers have the right to clean and safe workplaces including good physical, environmental, and moral conditions. Workers have the right to be informed of safety risks and instructed on how to follow the regulations and improve safety, including the right to protective clothing and equipment, first aid, health exams, and compensation for workplace injuries or sickness. By law workers have the right to remove themselves from situations that endanger their health and safety without jeopardizing their employment. No sectors or groups of workers, including those in the informal sector, are specifically exempted from these laws.

The Ministry of Labor is responsible for enforcing the minimum wage rates in the private sector, and the Ministry of Finance does so in the public sector. The ministries usually investigated violations of minimum wage rates only after workers lodged a complaint.

The Ministry of Labor did not effectively enforce minimum wage, hours of work, and OSH standards in the informal economy, since the Ministry of Labor only regulates the formal sector. The number of labor inspectors (135 in 2014) was not sufficient to enforce compliance. Agricultural workers were among the most vulnerable to poor work conditions and wage theft. The lack of frequent and enforced sanctions for violations created little deterrence for violations. Despite the relatively low number of inspectors, some businesses reported frequent visits by labor inspectors citing capricious violations and threats of fines in order to receive bribes.

There were few industrial jobs outside the Maputo area. The country's special economic and industrial areas have the same regulations for wages, workweek, and occupational safety and health as elsewhere. The Inspector General for Economic Activities, which is composed of representatives from a number of ministries, regulated these zones. There were no reports of violations of wage, overtime, or occupational safety and health standards in these special economic zones.